Hemang Domadia, born in Kolkata, began his journey into poetry at the tender age of 8. His early passion for words evolved into a profound exploration of his inner world. 3 A.M. delves into the intimate and raw thoughts that often rise during the quiet, introspective hours of the early morning.

3 A.M.

Hemang Domadia

Dedicated to those who think endlessly.

Introduction

3 a.m. is a strange and sacred hour—a time when the world feels both infinitely large and suffocatingly small. It's the hour of sleeplessness, when the weight of unspoken emotions finds its voice and thoughts, we'd rather bury claw their way to the surface.

 This book is my exploration of those moments— the restless nights and fragile dawns that leave us feeling both lost and found. Through poetry, I've tried to capture the loneliness, the longing, and the unexpected clarity that only the dark hours can bring.

Contents

Distanced Dance

Our world is a diamond

You are my shine, my gem

I found a friend to dance with at night

A laughter for whom I'd take a flight.

Remember that day in February?

You etched your name in my memory,

You became my remedy,

Making me wish we could be together for the
century.

We cry about the distance,

But are we really that far?

With coffee-stained letters, we share our
days,

In digital worlds where love and friendship
softly plays.

Every cup of tea we shared

Every picture of you I glared.

I wish we always remain paired,

In a bond, I've forever sworn.

And yes, I joke, I'd marry you, dear,

In our own little world, where nothing's
unclear.

You laugh and say, "You're ridiculous, true,

But honestly, I'd say yes to you."

So, if you allow me,

I'd love to invite you to this dance.

Until we a can create our DMs

Into laughter shared in a real-life glance.

4C 4F 56 45

In lines of code, our love brew,

Two programmers, just me and you.

A binary bond, a digital affection,

Flowcharts of sweet connection.

Love's syntax let their feelings show,

But errors it did throw.

In loops of longing, they compiled their dream,

Both found love in one another and a machine.

Hemang Domadia

Sunrise

How are sunrises free?

Not a coin, no fee,

There for all to see.

We don't need anyone to share it with.

Who lied about love's need?

We are enough.

You are enough.

I am enough.

Standing alone is not a loss.

Happiness is not with anyone's mind.

The world can spin,

While we can learn,

To let solitude happily burn,

Let our sun rise,

It's free,

If you dare to see.

Empty Seats

I can't fill the empty seats at the lunch table.

I sit alone.

Maybe it's my fault,

I can't keep them, they slip,

I'm grasping for something that was never there.

Am I the cause?

No one answers when I speak,

I am wrapped in my echoes.

Invisible, am I too much?

I try to fit and mould,

I'm wrong, I can't see,

A lie that I can't recognize,

I've become a shadow,

I built the space but I am the fault.

What Am I?

I met her on a Monday evening

The sky dim and wide

We shared the same bus stop

I stepped close

She smiled with a warm light

I wanted to talk tonight

The universe knew our roles

I looked in her eyes

Something beautiful, far and near

What if we stayed up all night

Lost till the morning's light

What is she that I'm falling so deep?

With her head on my chest she sleeps

Could this be forever

Her lips soft and divine

I want to say "I love you"

"Tell me if you feel the same"

She says,

3 A.M.

"I know you do. But what am I?"

"I know you do. But what am I?"

Midnight Serenade

In the moon's soft glow,

secrets did unfold,

In the late night,

our stories untold.

Her voice, a melody,

whispered in the night,

With each word spoken,

our souls took flight.

The world stood still,

time lost its reign,

Two hearts entwined,

no need to explain.

In that sacred moment,

vulnerability embraced,

In the late night,

love's grace interlaced.

Unfallen Grace

He fell first, but she never fell,

In the realm of love's beguiling spell,

He soared on wings of hope and desire,

She stood firm, heart untamed by fire.

He whispered sonnets, a poet's lament,

She listened, yet remained indifferent,

His heart bared open and true,

But hers stayed guarded, her walls held through.

In this tale of hearts, their paths diverged,

One entrapped, while the other surged,

He fell first, entangled in passion's embrace,

But she never fell, preserved in her own grace.

Château d'amour

I bought a castle in France, just like the one I built for you,

When I was two.

Our love story so early,

A fairy tale journey.

I built the bridge of fears,

A connection unbroken through tears.

Secret passages of joy,

Our adventure, two souls alloy.

Let's roam the halls, hand in hand,

Dance as our dreams expand.

I twirl you as you laugh in delight,

With you it all feels right.

The castle echoes our everlasting song,

It is where we belong.

Outcast?

they left me behind,

am I not their kind?

it killed me each day,

I saw them get away.

they went far too fast,

am I an outcast?

is it misunderstanding?

or just pure hating?

Cards

Cards on the table that we never got to play,

Two decks now tucked away.

Aces of laughter, bring our win,

Jokers of love, make us sin.

Queen of time,

King of hope, in his prime.

A sincere poker face we wore,

Our lives got shuffled more.

A gamble of love we play,

Chips of passion we might have to pay.

Hearts of love, spades of fear,

Diamonds of courage and the cloves bring us
near.

Pain Of Loving

Face with beauty overflowing,

I can never stop loving.

For your love I would feed flames,

With your hints you play games.

I hold my love unwilling to impart,

To confess, would wound your heart.

The pain of loving yet concealing,

The pain of loving yet not kneeling.

She's my beautiful girl, a secret bliss,

A tender ache and stolen kiss.

In my head you are mine,

In yours I am just another decline.

Hemang Domadia

An Expensive Drop

One drop of tear,

From the eye that saw too far,

That expensive drop, many fear,

Sign of the unhealing scar.

Unfulfilled dreams,

Seeds of hope, unsprouted,

Like autumn leaves,

Throws me grieved.

It wrecked my heart

The moon is new

Not a visible cart

No matter if gone are few...

Lover Boy

You haven't called me in a week,

My heart is bruised,

Too clingy? or am I a mess?

I wait for that buzz, that ringtone,

You know that I think of you more than you
think of me,

But you never asked.

You never asked me why I love you,

You never asked why I stole glances of you,

I never asked if I would ever be your centre
of gravity.

Hemang Domadia

Mirror Mirror

Mirror Mirror on the wall,

Who feels the smallest among all?

Worthy of love's comforting shawl,

But in this world of judgement can't stop the fall.

Mirror Mirror on the wall,

Who carries rejection's heavy ball?

All confidence shattered and solitude builds him a wall,

Each time he faces the world, he begins to stall.

Mirror Mirror on the wall,

Who was kicked down before standing tall?

Where did he go wrong? Can't recall.

When will he rise despite the fall?

Silenced

Silent screams lost in the abyss of darkness,

Unheard,

Unseen,

Suffocated.

Comforting hands now grasp in brutality,

Every gasp, every choked sob,

The undying will to break free.

Why does a cry for help fade into a void of forgotten promises?

Each cry turns into a roar,

In the roar of thousand voices,

Weight of silence is a stifling shroud.

When will change come?

Who will be the messenger?

Unseen

I found her when I was not looking for love

Where silence carries the sounds of the world

And whispers them to my heart

Unannounced she came

Like the soft dawn

Somehow, she fit right in my puzzle

Yet I wasn't looking in that corner

Was it a promise forever?

Or just a fleeting constellation?

A glimmer in the vastness

That made me wonder....

An Open Door

What do you want?

The door can either close or open.

Don't you want to take a chance?

Every word we don't speak,

Every silence we don't weight,

It's a jail I can't navigate.

I say do not go,

Yet I am the one who opens the door.

Yes?

or a, no?

The in between stings deep,

More than the scars you've carved.

Now that I close the door,

Your shadows move away.

Revive

I came to you

because you were supposed to bring me to
life

without me you grew?

Doesn't sharpness sting on the knife?

In your lazy pile of hay,

I linger, cast aside.

When I am lost and muted in the night

You wear delusions like jewels bright

Let that one-page turn

and whisper low

Let that fire burn

I'm here, stagnant and slow

Is it too late?

Can I revive?

Yes.

No.

Every truth be told.

Every heartbeat be bold.

Every second be sold.

Hemang Domadia

Lost

I can't see you anymore,

I can't see us anymore.

You sailed off to a distant shore.

The sun saw our laugh,

The moon our tears,

But now the ink is out,

The string broken,

A change in seasons.

A short distance used to feel like miles,

Now even miles feel short.

I wonder if you think of me,

If you remember me.

The flower that lost colour,

The time that lost ticks,

You will have a piece of me,

I might never meet the peace of us.

Relics

I was picked

Placed in your hand.

Everything felt right.

Each touch that left a mark

Is now forgotten.

Now I lie in your dusty memories,

Just a relic.

In the corner rusting in moist air,

Air so thin of your love,

I was a part of your story.

But now thrown in the depth of the night.

A victim of trust,

A reminder of love turned to fear.

Hemang Domadia

Till Death Do Us Part

Hi,

Hi,

And after five more awkward hi's,

I felt a strong, "Friends till we die"

A spark that softly grew,

Every night I spent with you.

Our stories and secrets,

Forever and always till the sun sets.

Every smile we cried,

Every tear we laughed.

Our love grew strong,

And friendship wrote a familial song.

A journey so messy and bright,

Everything just so perfectly right.

For this is our delicate race,

You are my beautiful space.

Hemang Domadia

The Girl Across the Street

You shine before the sun,

You glow under the moon.

I see you dance to tunes each morning,

In the quiet of this screaming distance.

I feel those butterflies,

As pretty as you.

But unaware that when you smile,

I feel the world could meet its doom without
a cry.

The first afternoon we talked,

I stood there enchanted,

In a bliss of awe,

In a fear of falling.

Across the street I see you,

Through my tiny window,

You steal my blinks,

Every time you look into mine.

The Winner That Failed

I want to cry,

I won the battle of failure.

Dreams are frozen in a burning future.

The weight of guilty chains,

I can't bear.

I ask for air,

But I am caught in this inner storm.

My castles crumble with every passing tide.

Within ashes,

I see my guiding star die.

Fading

You remembered to forget me.

But forgot how we,

Invested clocks for each other,

The same from a different mother.

You chase the sun,

I observe you behind the flowers,

You a star on the rise,

I am but unseen in your eyes.

Each word from you feels like a gift,

I feel lonely as we drift,

I scroll up to the past,

The time when I wasn't the outcast.

I hang a gallery of you on my wall,

I did not want this fall,

But you sent your unread reply,

You are fading and I wonder why.

Dust

In a crowded room

I sat empty

Ghosts of my laugh

Haunt my tears

Each second so heavy

All that is left of me

Is a withered rose in a vase of tears

The petals of my soul

Fall as the years pass by

Dark corners call my name

Answered by the light I lost

I am now dust.

I am now left behind.

Hemang Domadia

My Someone

In you I see me,

In me I can't see without you.

You are my mirror,

Me your shadow.

When the lows are tall,

Or the highs are short.

I'll be your shelter,

I'll be your stage.

When you ache,

I feel your sweet pain.

I'll walk with you,

I'll talk to you.

I'd stop for you,

I'd top every mountain.

I live and die,

For every moment we live.

So hey,

Never alone will you be,

3 A.M.

Never a tear you shall shed without shoulder.

Every smile we embrace,

Every frown will fit right in place.

Please tell me all of it,

Please let me be by your lows and hits.

You are my someone,

You are my everyone.

Talk

"Talk to someone"

They tell me,

To talk to someone.

But who?

They tell me

I am not alone.

Who is with me?

Nobody.

I spend hours waiting

and wailing.

Someone will come,

I just need one

Person to talk to.

One,

Human to smile with.

One day,

without negativity on my mind.

If I come to an end,

Tears will dry soon.

If I become great,

Smiles will fade soon.

I am non-existent.

Every second I get more distant.

Now when someone smiles,

I feel dull.

I feel everyone is here,

Just to someday leave,

For some better belief,

Everyone is my friend,

But none am I.

Hemang Domadia

Mine

I love her,

She is my soul,

My heart,

My affections,

MINE.

I dance to the music of her voice;

Her eyes sparkle like the gem she is.

She is a radiant glow.

In her presence time falters,

The world fades.

Each moment is a canvas

Where love finds its way.

Her hair is a story untold,

Her spirit a melody,

In perfect harmony.

She captures my air,

For when the prettiest girl

Looks at me,

My heart drops,

My eyes pop,

Butterflies hop,

and I just love her lots.

Hemang Domadia

A Ghost

I was addicted to you.

I was used,

and used to being with you.

With you loneliness felt like

a crowd of warmth and comfort.

We said "forever",

But I always feared the end.

I knew this chaotic comfort

was just a silent symphony

of sweet betrayal.

I am now lost in the maze of laughs

and the puzzle of memories.

We were one bond,

Now, I am one alone.

I still stand on top

of the monument of "forever".

The ghost of our friendship,

Sings the songs of brokenness.

While I learn to erase lines of you

I marked in ink.

Hemang Domadia

Thousand Miles

A thousand miles beneath the sun,

My heart shall never die,

For love I take this solemn vow,

You have all of me, here and now.

For you I'd pluck,

The moon from heaven,

Trade my spirit,

For a cost not too high.

Every tear,

Every cheer,

I'll walk for you through the fear,

So, you can feel the troubles clear.

I'll shout your name forever,

Like Romeo for his Giulietta.

Let the world conspire.

Let the world scream.

I dare to dream,

A thousand miles,

To find her in my arms,

To hold you close, a true charm.

Nobody

HER:

Nobody stays forever,

I have seen it in the fading light,

In every heart that's wandered

And every love that slips from sight.

ME:

But I'd stay a moment longer,

If only for a smile or two.

Even if time's hands grow stronger,

I'd be the nobody here with you.

HER:

A nobody? But that's no place to stand

In shadows where the lonely fade.

Why would you choose such hollow land

Where promises break and hopes are laid?

3 A.M.

ME:

For nobody stays forever,

But in that fleeting breath, I'll be true.

I'll stand where the world may sever,

Only to be the silence after you.

HER:

The silence? What is there to find

In silence, where words won't grow?

I would rather the noise, the knotted brain

Than nothing where there's space to spread

ME:

Perhaps you'd say it was emptiness,

Then, in that room, I'll hold the light,

I'll be the echo in your stress,

A soft reflection in your night.

HER:

But don't you fear the passing tide?

Love that, flickers and goes black,

Can you stand the storm inside,

When the waves grow big and sink inside?

ME:

Fear is a friend I know too well,

But I'll walk with it if you'll hold my hand.

In every fall, we rise or fell,

But in your glance, I'll understand.

HER:

But what if you fall alone

The ground so far beneath your feet?

Would you still want to be unknown,

And leave the world with no retreat?

ME:

Perhaps it's not a fall at all,

Or standing tall, or feeling weak.

But knowing I gave my all,

Even when there's no one left to speak.

HER:

Then you'd be nobody?

A shadow with no claim to fame?

Nobody stays forever, you know.

ME:

I'll be your nobody then,

Just for the moments we can weather,

In your eyes, I'll live again.

HER:

A nobody... but maybe that's a start,

A name that doesn't need to last.

I'd be fine with a stolen heart,

If only time could move more fast.

ME:

In the quiet of the leaving hour,

It'll be me who casts a shadow by your side,

Not one bound by forever but by the power

Of love that needs never to hide.

HER:

So, we'll be nobody's, for now and here,

And though it ends, I'll feel no pain.

Perhaps, possibly, my love,

We're more than nobody if we stay.

ME:

Nobody stays forever,

But I'll be yours just the same—

Not forever, but whatever,

In the fleeting, I'll stake my claim.

Dear Bestie

Please let me be,

The one you'll forever see

A constant flame

Not just a game.

You laugh with a glow

But your heart has someone else to show

Yet I keep smiling

I can't help but think something...someone is going

I try to hold on, but my grip slips through

How quickly

How quietly

I am replaced by you.

Not Worthy

I'm sorry I met you.

I am not worthy for your stay.

Your life would've been flowers of May,

Without me by you.

I thought I could lift you,

Make you shine,

But I tangled you in my broken lifeline.

You deserve someone whole,

Someone pure.

Not me,

Who can't even be sure

Of the future I bring,

Will it smile or sting?

I'm sorry.

Sorry indeed.

I cry for what I have done.

I'm sorry I met you,

Your life would've been

So much better without

Me in it.

I'm sorry I met you,

Your life would've been

Hemang Domadia

No One Except Her

No one except her

Forever.

No matter what,

I will always return to her.

Only her.

I loved her long before today

She breaths in my chest.

She is what my eyes seek.

She resides in my head and then my heart.

The days change,

The world spins,

The seasons come and go,

But this love is not just for show.

It's her.

I dream of her,

I dream if she dreams of me.

Her name will never leave my soul.

For her, I will stand,

None except her hand in my hand.

Hemang Domadia

Holy Inferno

I am lost

in your sinful maze.

Your gaze

makes me a Satan and saint.

Your touch-burns like the flames of sin.

A devil in angel's grace.

Lips that curse the sacred,

Your love is salvation and despair.

You make the devil pray,

and the Gods prey.

You are a holy blasphemy,

an unholy peace.

You make clouds of gold,

cry like storms.

A love that is

neither good nor ill.

An evil with halo bright,

walking the sacred light.

3 A.M.

I am the angel who wants your dark,

The saint who bears Satan's mark.

Be Kind

The alarms chime,

Playing the chain of time.

Fingers dipped in coffee,

Notes feel anomaly.

Craving.

Carving.

Creating.

Competing for excellence.

Every score is an identity,

A crown of the witty.

Smiles are grey,

Friends are away,

The prefect pressure,

Gives everyone except him pleasure.

Late mornings and early nights,

Like a robot he fights,

The urge to crumble.

Killed by the smallest fumble.

Born to shine?

I just want to be kind.

Opposite

I am late, you are already there.

Saying you were extra early while you pull a
chair.

I watch you sip coffee, I watch your eyes,

Sipping the tea of love from my life.

You organize it all from A to Z.

I've scattered my things-pizza boxes and
paper cups, forgotten debris.

I text you fast, you think before saying the
right.

But still, you never believe that you are my
type.

I binge the shows you've read,

Your favourite quotes highlighted in my
head.

3 A.M.

We contradict, you and I,

But we love till the stars fall from the sky.

57

Hemang Domadia

The Book and The Pen

Every page you left a mark,

Every line you wrote.

You would reach for me in the quite

and write stories of us.

You would ink your secrets,

as if the world could never tear us apart.

But now,

you found a new book.

The pen no longer lives among my pages,

for I've been written till the very end.

You never visit me,

You never try to find any blank space.

I remember everything you told me,

I have it all.

I gather the dust of being forgotten,

and the spiderwebs of being replaced.

Pages of the past don't interest the pen.

The pen has no reason to return.

But I am just a book.

Waiting but not wanting to be forgotten.

In A Room Full of People

A needle in a haystack,

The warmth of winter,

The rainbow in black,

A ripple in the oceans.

Your presence is easy to find.

I don't need directions,

I know where you are.

I'll find you in spaces where others would miss,

The golden kiss.

You are the answer

To my unspoken quest

You make my blind,

In a crowd you are all I find.

Now

We have the rest of our lives,

to chase the wind.

Let's go to that quiet place,

beneath all the haste,

where time is honey,

slow and sweet in taste.

Not sure what I was doing before.

Not sure what I will do tomorrow.

Life is not bound by hours or minutes,

Urgency extends to infinites.

Patience, the present

is a garden we are afraid of.

Wait for every petal to bloom,

not because it is soon,

but because it is right.

The journey is a gift.

Enjoy it without the burden of soon,

soon is never now,

now is all we have.

Be alive,

Be aware,

Breathe the moments before they slip away.

Christmas Eve

Christmas eve December,

When you held my hand,

Cold winds through my coat,

A frozen heart no one sees.

Lights on the street red, blue and green,

None of them shine for me,

I search for warmth,

Only to find bitter memories in winter's glaze.

I want to be the star on the tree,

Santa's forgotten list is all I could be,

No love, no touch,

No gentle kiss.

A season of joy sold,

The night I held my own hand,

It's Christmas eve December,

But love is still a stone.

64

Confession

I whispered,

I mixed in the vivid air,

A fragile truth.

Yes, I told her

I watched her smile fade

She looked

She paused

With words she turned the summer cold

I blinked at her

I saw her warm soul turn snow

My silent scream stuck inside

A cut that didn't hurt but killed

I ruined it

I confessed love

I cannot pay the price

I cannot make it up to her

So, I'll quietly love her from far
A fading star
A fading story
A fading friendship.

www.ingramcontent.com/pod-product-compliance
Lightning Source LLC
Chambersburg PA
CBHW031328130726

47988CB00007B/3040